The Plan

An Addict's Guide To Freedom

By: Corey Robbins

2019

Table of Contents

Introduction

Sometimes the only way we know how to define a thing is to say what it is not. In most cases, doing this doesn't bring us any closer to what that thing is. This book will offer a non-scientific, yet highly qualified and informed perspective on what it means to be addicted, what it means to overcome addiction, what it means to still live as an addict, and some ways through which this overcoming can be achieved.

To the initiated, feelings like guilt, shame, regret, loss, and hopelessness have woven their way through different parts of our using life. Rather than fill this book with a detailed account of the particulars from my personal experience that underscore such negativity, we will consider the subject of addiction from a universal viewpoint. This simply means that addiction has no prejudice. It has no bias. Suffice it to say, I've done more than some, less than others, but plenty enough for me. If there is one way that people from opposite ends of the socioeconomic spectrum can relate, it is through addiction. As such, some of the means by which our power over this state can be restored apply to us all as well.

This book is intended to serve as a source that will uplift, inspire, and perhaps provide a sense of hope to those who feel lost. For those of you who are currently addicted to substance of any kind, some of this material may prove helpful, and some may not. I encourage you to apply the suggestions in the chapters you find valuable and leave the rest behind. For those of you who are not addicts but closely acquainted with someone who is, the same applies. Some of the principles contained herein may help you to better understand your loved one's struggle, and more importantly, how you may help them conquer that struggle.

The content offered provides an adaptable framework. A specific sequence is not required. In fact, it is advised that the reader create a structure of their own. For some, all of the guidelines will prove beneficial; for others only a few. To be sure, there is something here for EVERYone. If the reader comes away finding only one of the chapters useful to their unique situation, the book will have served its purpose. The concepts presented are simple. However, any combination thereof, performed with repetition, furthers the shift in the balance of power that the addicted is ultimately in search of.

Anyone who knows what it means for their DNA to launch an all-out attack on any attempt at moderation, this book is for you. Anyone who is intimate with the Siren Song of their inner demons, this book is for you. Anyone who desires deeply to live a life of their own creation, and to Carpe that motherfucking Diem, this book is for you. This book is a guide, let it lead you to freedom.

Corey Robbins
Franklin, TN
2019

Ritual

As addicts, part of our high comes in the performance of rituals. Each of us has a unique process we follow when using. We romanticized the taste, smell, feel, and sound of the experience. During these intense moments of craving, we are extremely present. All of our attention is brought to bear upon even the slightest detail of the process leading up to the satisfaction we are about to experience. We are as much addicted to the ritual of using as we are to the substance itself.

As it happens, rituals can be used to our advantage. It may help to think of a ritual as a psychological anchor of sorts. Old destructive rituals must be replaced with new and healthy ones. It is through this replacement that we are able to sustain our recovery, and more smoothly navigate the beginning of this recovery. Without a concentrated effort on new rituals, the power and lure of the old remains, making it ever more difficult for our recovery to gain traction.

Rituals act as pieces of the scaffolding in the necessary framework within which we must operate sometimes from one minute to the next. The creation of new rituals does not need to be complex. In fact, it's best if things are kept simple. Start by making a list of the things that are done on a daily basis. The objective is to replace destructive behaviors with productive habits. Through daily repetition, we reinforce the new rituals and begin to internalize new behavioral patterns that move our lives in a positive direction.

So we understand each other, I am not suggesting that making your bed will bring the same level of gratification as did the consumption of your drug of choice. However, the effect of the formation of new rituals is cumulative. By bringing the same level of presence that we have while using to the seemingly trivial activities of our day, our awareness begins to expand.

In the early days of recovery, we are way out of our comfort zone. Chaotic as our old comfort zone may have been, it was what we were used to; madness was normal. By selecting a few things to do each day at the exact same time in the exact same way, we were able to restore our sense of safety and achieve a feeling of productivity.

Relative to what follows, detox is easy. Withdrawal from any substance or addictive behavior is accompanied by discomfort. In some cases, extreme discomfort. Please allow me this brief digression. Let's use opiates for an example. During the first one to three days of withdrawal, a person can experience the most acute and brutal physical pain they have ever known. It is relentless. Vomiting and diarrhea are a constant. It is not uncommon to go a few days without sleep. The word craving takes on an entirely new meaning. At this point, the addiction is fighting for its life, the agony is peaking, and the body is screaming for even the slightest bit of relief. Successfully negotiating this excruciating period is no small feat; however, comparatively speaking, it is easy.

Because now the real challenge begins. Now that we have overcome the physical component to our addiction, we must in essence relearn how to live. We have if not forever, hopefully at least for the foreseeable future just said goodbye to our closest companion. So while the physical effects may have diminished, thus freeing us from the required maintenance, the psychological and emotional complexity has just begun. And this is precisely the point at which the implementation of new rituals would be of such value.

This is also the point at which so many of us remain mired in our old habitual ways of thinking. As mentioned, keeping things simple is best, at least in the beginning. For some, this may be difficult. Here I will make a few suggestions that you are free to put in place, or just use to get the wheels turning.

Waking up at the same time each day is a great ritual to practice. Ideally, this would be earlier rather than later. It may seem like nothing, but even forcing yourself out of the bed when you would prefer to hit snooze five times is a small victory. So you are able to face and overcome a challenge, which sets the tone for the day and gives you momentum. It is important also to be conscious of it in this way. Again, bringing presence to these new behaviors will help to engrain them quicker, fortifying the reserve of strength that will be called upon countless times throughout the early days of recovery.

Next, make the bed. Our existence has just been turned on its head, and the act of making the bed provides a sense of order that we control. Making the bed also serves as another small victory in our morning, thereby adding to the momentum. A successful morning carries the day. Tiny as these two acts may seem, entering the day with a feeling of accomplishment creates a substantial shift in attitude.

Another positive ritual to practice is writing your thoughts after waking. Write about any subject of your choosing. It can but does not have to be about anything specific. Just let your thoughts wander where they will. In its infancy, recovery comes with a flood of feelings. We are waking up, coming to life. One of the healthiest ways to process this experience is by writing. I would like to reiterate that this need not be structured in any way. Let your emotions fill the page. This exercise is meant to be cathartic. Transferring your thoughts and feelings onto the page is a useful way to release any negativity that you may be holding onto as well as express gratitude for all of the positive things happening in your life.

It is easy to overlook the role that rituals play and the power they have in our lives. These are only a few suggestions to help you get started. Please use them or others of your own making so that you can begin to understand their efficacy and value in creating a better life.

Passion

The word passion conjures many different ideas, but for the purposes of this book, it is interchangeable with the notion of purpose. Addiction can be fueled in some cases by the sense of aimlessness that governs our existence. We drift through life with no understanding of why it is we are here. Or perhaps worse, we know what we want to do but are unable to make it happen. Each of us has a unique capability that is exclusively our own. We are each equipped with something that is exclusive to us.

In keeping with the theme of simplicity, we are reminded that this unique capability may not be something that will have a global reach. It can be small; it can be something that may not generate much in the way of money. Nevertheless, it brings you both great pleasure and a sense of direction and purpose. For those of you who do not know what your passion is, or have never felt called to anything specific, listen more closely. It is there, you must pay attention. For those of you who do have a passion, but have either quit pursuing or never even bothered to pursue it because a blueprint for its monetization has not appeared, forget about the money.

Settling for less is a byproduct of a world which conditions us to let our pragmatic voice override our desire to pursue that which makes us happy. As addicts, we are using a substance or behavior to either fill a hole or numb a wound that won't heal. Having a passion eliminates the feeling of void and diverts our attention away from past hurt. When our minds are clear, focusing on those things to which we are naturally inclined becomes easier. What is more, we become receptive to the idea that it is alright to follow such inclinations. Whereas before we may have disregarded them, or perhaps been unaware of them altogether.

Passion places emphasis on something bigger than us, it allows us to get out of our own heads at least for a little while. Our focus is put on something that gives us a sense of direction, a sense of meaning. Passion provides a mechanism through which we can express our impulses and explore a part of ourselves that has been neglected. Pouring ourselves into something provides a vehicle whereby we may transcend the limitations imposed by the mental framework of addiction.

As with the other suggested methods in this book, this one need not be grandiose. If yours is not a passion that moves and speaks to the spirit of the world, that is completely fine. If it is, then great. The point is to pour yourself into an activity with the same effort as you did your addiction. It may also be beneficial for this effort to be something that can be tracked. If you can make incremental improvements in something that you love, you can get a feeling of gratification that is healthy, which improves the chances of remaining free from destructive patterns and behaviors.

Making progress in an area of life that we are passionate about, fills the space that we have tried filling with our addiction in a way that is beneficial. In some cases, at the root of our addiction are found feelings of self-doubt, and many other negative emotions which are the catalyst for self-destructive behaviors. Discovering a pursuit for which we have a great deal of passion can replace those negative feelings with a sense of self-worth. Replace the old feelings, and you replace the old behaviors as well.

We don't have to set out to change the world, only ourselves. As it happens, the single best way to change the world is to change ourselves, because when we change ourselves, we do indeed change the world. Having a passion is the quickest way to transform into the person we were always meant to be.

The word passion is interchangeable with mission, calling, purpose, or anything else that describes what it is you feel that you are meant to do. I believe that this principle is the most important in the journey to freedom from addiction. Being able to see improvement in an area of our lives that holds meaning is far more gratifying than a high from any addiction.

People fall into one of three categories in terms of knowing what they are passionate about. The first are those who have always known what they love to do, but a commitment to serving the needs of the beast have for a period of time been overridden. The second are those who have had a curiosity about one or many things but never devoted much energy toward any of them. The third are those who simply have no idea what to do, or even know what they want to do.

For those of us struggling with addiction, and continuously heeding the call of the voice of the inner demon, discovering a passion can be especially difficult. In the very beginning of sobriety, we experience an overwhelming flood of emotion. It is crucial that we pay close attention to what these emotions are telling us. We are waking up to the person we are supposed to be. In this time of heightened awareness, it is important that we not ignore the impulses that we feel. By not shutting out our natural inclination, we may discover a path to pursue. The quicker we start to devote our energy to an aim that could bring us fulfillment, the greater the chances we have for remaining free of addiction. Life can be difficult enough as it is, never mind the perils of addiction, and learning to live without being addicted. Whether you call it passion, purpose, calling, mission or anything else, my hope is that you let one find you. Having a passion can mitigate to a large degree the aimlessness that accompanies any addiction, and the void left when we become free. Often we are unaware of how much energy we put into our career as an addict.

Countless hours have gone into the evasion of suspicion of friends, family, coworkers, neighbors, and everyone else we come into contact with. Just imagine what could be accomplished if that same effort were applied to an end that was healthy and useful to ourselves as well as others. Start small, and know that by so doing, you are on your way to something much bigger.

Exercise

The most immediate way to get out of your head is to get into your body. Doing something physical produces instant ROI. It can be something as simple as getting down, and doing as many pushups as possible. In fact, if you are someone who does not regularly frequent the gym, this is the best place to start. During the initial stages of recovery, do not go sign up for a membership at your local gym. The percentage of people who sign up and then never go is staggering. Start right where you stand.

Do some sit-ups, pushups, or some jumping jacks. Anything to increase your heart rate. Physical exertion collects our focus faster than anything else. Any mental fog will dissipate with an increased heart rate. A faster pulse introduces a set of biochemical responses that are far beyond the scope of this book. Suffice it to say, for addicts especially, exercise is crucial to freedom. I say, especially because exercising produces chemicals in the brain that make us feel good. Most importantly, it happens immediately.

And as addicts, instant gratification through behavior or substance is something that we are quite fond of, but that has become detrimental to our existence. Through exercise, we can achieve the same feel good in a way that is much more conducive to our survival. When we were using, the thought of quitting even if we wanted to was too painful. So we would just continue to use. Then, whether it was through the power of something within ourselves, or the power of external forces, we managed to put one day between us and our addiction. Suddenly, there was a glimmer of hope. One day turned into two, then three. A week has passed, and depending on your drug of choice, you found yourself on the other end of the gauntlet.

How does this relate to exercise? In the same way we found ourselves filled with pain at the mere thought of quitting, we experience nearly the same feeling when we think about any type of exercise regimen. Even decathletes have to overcome that voice that tells them it is alright to skip a day. Beginning to exercise is very difficult. Similar to kicking, once we manage one day, we find the next to be if not easy, not quite as hard.

Naturally, as addicts, once we feel the feelings that exercising provides, we want more. Exercise, once turned into a habit, has a tendency to carry over into other areas of life. Exercising regularly translates into positive psychological and emotional benefits as well as physical. As you begin to feel better physically, you begin to feel better mentally. By overcoming the impulse to follow the path of least resistance, we gain a psychological advantage. This advantage is then applied to other things in life that we have to deal with.

Being able to draw upon a reserve of strength from the accumulation of small wins is sometimes the difference between continuing on the path of freedom and falling back into destructive behavior patterns. The exercise cycle is self-fulfilling in that when you exercise, you feel better. When you feel better, you have more energy to devote to the areas of your life in which you want to make progress. Once you begin to move the needle in these areas of life that hold value for you, you feel good. This of course leads to more exercise, which of course leads to more progress and so on. You do not have to be conscious of this process, just trust and know that this is what is going on beneath the surface.

Again, I understand that the thought of starting to exercise can be daunting, which is why I said to start where you stand. In the beginning, make it short and simple. Do not rehearse in your mind how difficult it will be to sign up for a membership at the gym, and the time it will take to get there, and what time it will be when you get home. This is the quickest way to ensure that you never do anything. You have everything you need right now, which is your own body. In this particular instance, having an addictive personality may actually serve you well. Because once you manage a string of days where you have done ten pushups, or ten jumping jacks, or ten sit-ups, or walked around the cul-de-sac, you will find yourself naturally wanting to increase these numbers, thus initiating the cascade of positive actions that lead to a healthy mental state.

By starting as small as possible, you are setting yourself up for success. It is alright if you are not drenched in sweat after each workout in the very beginning. The key is to overcome the internal dialogue that is telling you that you will start the next day. The next day always turns into the next day. Just as it did when we were trying to kick. Same voice different goal. What is the point of ten pushups? Simply to do them. Rewiring our brain is really what we are after. What makes exercise so effective is the immediacy in the reward.

Knowing what to do and doing what we know is common among everyone. We all know that exercise is good for us, and we all know that we should do it. For addicts especially, exercise can be the shortest bridge between intense craving and possible relapse and continued freedom. Understanding that starting to exercise can be challenging, we have looked at ways in which to reduce the most friction between ourselves and actually doing it. Ultimately, there is nothing left except simply to do it.

If you are someone who has managed any substantial interval of separation (by substantial I mean even 24 hours) between yourself and the addictive substance or behavior, you have clearly demonstrated the necessary strength of will required to start an exercise regimen of any kind. Be it pushups or an Ironman contest. I mean this sincerely. Kicking is hard. It is terrifying. If you've done it, you've proved that you possess an uncommon strength. If you haven't *yet,* know that you possess this strength as well. Exercise can be the catalyst to unlocking this strength.

Spirit

I am calling this next section Spirit. Some may refer to the same power as God, consciousness, divine intelligence, the unified field, or a number of other names. Also, I realize that there is a percentage of people with whom this section will not resonate because of their belief in the nonexistence of such a presence. This section is not meant to challenge or change your current belief.

If you are someone who has dealt with addiction, and you are reading this, then we can at the very least acknowledge that for a time there was a power greater than ourselves which controlled our lives. While feeding our addiction, we often have an extremely external locus of control. It is commonly our misperception that we are victims of a malignant force that is plotting against us at every turn. Little do we realize that it is we who are acting against ourselves. This is certainly not to say that bad things only happen to people who are addicted, but by virtue of our lifestyle, we attract some of the darker elements of life.

Being human comes with an inherent inquisitiveness. The foundation for this section is that there is something bigger than us, that there is something more to this experience than can be seen. By being open to exploring ideas of the mystical, metaphysical, and divine, we at the very least give ourselves permission to think about what is beyond. For an addict, this can be quite beneficial. We need to be taken out of our own head; we need to know that we are not the center of all things. Our problems are magnified and intensified when we are using.

We feel bad, so we use, then we feel worse because we used, which makes us use again. This cycle is called vicious for good reason. It compounds. How does Spirit play into this? Spirit is a force into which all of this can be released. Spirit does not need to be fed; it simply needs to be acknowledged. Spirit is there for us to cultivate a relationship that will be supportive in some of life's challenging times. This association is conducive to a healthy life. We are not turning our old view, the one where we saw the world plotting against our every more, on its head.

Rather, we now understand that we are at the helm of our life, and that Spirit is a source of strength. Of course, we are each free to define Spirit however we choose. From ancient traditions to the New Age, there is something for everyone. I would caution against rigidity, it is counterproductive and imposing. What we have with Spirit is personal. It is there for us to draw upon when needed. When we become free from addiction, life goes on. The same things that triggered us to use are still there. We can remove ourselves from some of these environments, but inevitably there are things that we can't avoid, which in the past may have led us to use.

The more we recognize Spirit in our lives, the deeper the connection. The stronger the awareness, the stronger the bond. What is the point in cultivating a deep bond in something for which there is no empirical evidence? Believing in something larger than ourselves can help to put our ego in check, and make us feel that we are part of something larger. This can be especially useful for addicts whose problems often are magnified by addictive behavior.

By reducing the size of our problems in our own head, we reduce the likelihood that we will fall back into addictive patterns to cope with them. The next time you are experiencing a particularly difficult situation, gaze up into the night sky. Hold your problem up to the incomprehensible grandeur of the cosmos. Pretend it is a mirror. Is there any reflection of your trouble? Can you see it at all? Does this exercise shrink the size of your worry to any extent? I am not delusional. I realize that throughout the course of life, we encounter extreme difficulty and heartbreak, much of which has no logical explanation.

However, a great deal of the things that most people worry about never even happen. And an addict's logic takes a minor issue and magnifies it into a major crisis. Spirit provides a mechanism through which all of that can be released. We can turn all of that angst over to something much greater than ourselves. But some may ask, isn't this just the inverse of the addict's victimhood mentality? I say that it is not. When we are addicted, the behavior or substance sometimes convinces us that we are unique in our suffering, that we have been singled out. With even a slight interval of separation from our addiction, we recognize how absurd this is.

What an acknowledgment of Spirit gives us is an understanding that we have agency; that we each have something within us that can contribute not only to a better life for ourselves but for those we care for, and who care for us. For some, science is Spirit. And for this group, slowly but surely through the application of the scientific method, the answers to existence will continue to be revealed. This notion of Spirit is applicable even for those of you in this group. Because the universe is kind of big, and while we may have gained some insight into its contents and origin, there are still a few things left to figure out before our total understanding is complete.

There is another group that stares up at the cosmos and wonders what may lie beyond. Their conception of this existence is one for which no concrete explanation can be given, and perhaps for this reason they believe that there is something else at work, something more than can be perceived through the senses. The aim of this essay is not to support either side of the belief spectrum, but to illustrate the favorable effects in the exploration of what I have referred to as Spirit for those of us who have lived with addiction. We are all familiar with Google Maps.

I have turned the function of this app into a philosophy of sorts which I have found to be quite effective at times. It works like this. In Maps, you can type in an address, and in most cases see a picture of this location up close. In an instant, you can take this view and zoom out so that your view is now from space. When I am in the middle of a trying time, I consider this to be the street view. In my mind, I will zoom out to shift my perspective of my problem.

Again, I realize that this is not always easy to do. Sometimes life can turn into such a shit storm from which we are unable to shift our perspective to anything else. It takes practice. It will never be perfect. What is? First, we must get to the point that we are conscious of being overwhelmed by our trouble. Then we must zoom out, and consider whether or not we will even remember this problem five years, five weeks, or five days from now. By zooming out, we are able to make what is giving us so much trouble a little smaller if even for a moment. Which as we know, in times past was all that came between us and getting high. That is precisely what this section—and this whole book for that matter—aims to do. I want to share some of the actions that I have used to fill the gap of the desire to get high, and actually getting high. Zooming out allows me to consider life's troubles as Spirit might view them. Because there are certain moments when all we can do is turn what is in our heart and our head over to a presence greater than ourselves.

Epilogue

At the time of this writing, I have lived as an addict free from addiction for the last fourteen years. Some of the more challenging times of my life have come during this period. Without question, the most beautiful times of my life have come during this period. At various points along the journey, I have relied on each of the ideas explored in this book. It has not always been easy, sometimes it has been extremely hard. When I was high, the thought of having to deal with the difficulties of life on my own and while sober was unimaginable.

Now, having lived free from addiction, it is impossible to imagine missing out on all of the great things that have happened in my life because of addiction. Not to mention the very real possibility that all the amazing experiences which have shown up in my life may never have happened had I continued living as I did.

Best I can see, there are four groups of addicts. For some, addiction is a bunch of ballyhoo, balderdash, bombast, bollocks, blarney, and the like. They are convinced that they can *handle* their shit. For some, there is a high degree of suspicion that they have lost the upper hand, but are not yet at the point of capitulation. For some, there is no question that shit is completely out of hand and that they are totally helpless when it comes to a certain behavior or substance. If you fall into the first group and happen to be reading this, I hope something herein has delivered a Chuck Norris roundhouse moment of clarity. If you fall into the second group, I hope this reading nudged you into the realization that the change you feel you need to make is indeed necessary. If you find yourself part of the third group, I hope you are taking immediate steps toward freedom.

Lastly, there are some of us who have traversed the full spectrum and have resumed our journey to becoming the actualized people we were always meant to be. Wherever you may currently find yourself on this path, it is my sincere hope that you have found something useful in this book. I hope that you have found something applicable and actionable to living a life free from addiction. In most cases, addiction is something that we gradually ease into over time. We follow a certain pattern of behavior and wake up one day to find that our entire existence has been turned on its head.

Unfortunately, there is no way to ease out of addiction. We have to sever our relationship with a certain behavior or substance cold turkey, full stop. It is hard. If you have not yet kicked, it will be one of the most difficult things you have to do. If you have, you know what I'm talking about. In my experience, practicing the things laid out in this book made the process of kicking, and eventually living free from addiction suck less. At a certain point, which is different for everybody, living free from addiction not only doesn't suck but actually becomes quite amazing. Of course, we still must live and deal with all of the complexities that are a part of life.

But those complexities are no longer compounded by an addiction. Instead of a downward spiral, the trajectory of our lives is trending upward. The law of compounding works when we are doing well also. The positive reinforcement we feel through the application of healthy habits is the fuel to continuing on a productive path. This way of life builds on itself, returning dividends daily, and the gains we make in momentum yield a sense of wellbeing that each of us craves. Addiction is a subject on which extensive literature exists.

This book has been purposely kept short, and its contents simplified. The reason for this is to ensure the least amount of resistance between knowing and doing. Deciding to free yourself from an addiction is a sort of surrender. This means we must be led. We are extremely fragile, especially in the early days of recovery. The slightest upset can set us back, each time usually being worse than the last. So we need early wins right away.

We need a few select actions that we can rely upon to give us definitive positive results. Along the way, we may have stopped using only to pick it up again at some later time. We have tried, but nothing to date has seemed to stick. This book makes no promises, there is no magic cure. But there is also no other choice but to keep trying *until.* Yes, but how do we do what we know we should? Who knows? The fact is that someone else having found a way to live free of addiction means that we can as well. Sometimes when we are having a difficult time, many well-meaning people in an attempt to make us feel better will say "it could be worse." This has never made me feel any better because, if knowing that it could be worse is meant to make me feel better, then knowing that it could be better makes me feel worse. And it could be better, much much better.

Life is hard enough without all of the bullshit that goes along with addiction. Addiction is one hell of a force. As with anything overwhelming, an effective approach is to deconstruct the issue into parts that are smaller than the whole. By doing this, we restore hope where none remains. There are of course many other means by which many other people have attained freedom from addiction. The concepts in this little book are few and simple on purpose. The last thing anyone consumed with addiction needs is for their escape to be made more difficult. It is at this point that other authors might convey uncertainty as to whether or not these principles will work for everyone. Not me. As I mentioned from the start, there is something in here for everyone. I realize that this is a bold claim. But it's made in complete confidence. A confidence that is informed both by my personal experience, as well as the observation of the successful application of these principles in the lives of others. I am not saying that it is or will be easy. It is very very hard.

The value of a thing is defined by the difficulty in its attainment. What is your life worth to you? That is what is at stake. Both quantitatively and qualitatively. If you are addicted to something, it is a definite possibility that your time may be limited. What is more, you will continue to experience unnecessary suffering. Ultimately, living free from addiction is up to us, and only us. Many are certainly ready and willing to help, but it must always begin with our own desire to be free. No amount of tough love will ever be enough to override our own decision to continue the path we're on or to choose another.

The choice to live free of addiction is one that has major implications on your life. Of course this is obvious, but our inclination is to focus on all of the things that we are giving up, which causes distress. It requires unvarnished brutal self-honesty. This personal inventory can be extremely painful yet healing. After we examine all of the things we are giving up, we can then turn our attention to everything we will gain.

For example, when we consider the relationships we have while using, we discover that the deepest bond in some cases is bondage. Once this becomes clear, it is easier to let these associations go so that we can form new, more meaningful ties based on who we truly are. As with most things in life, what we truly value is what we have earned. You must earn this, and when you do, you will hold it as one of the things you value most. In the very early stages of my own freedom from addiction, I used to think that simply giving up drugs and alcohol could not be the main achievement of my life.

Now I realize that by releasing my commitment to addiction, I gave myself permission to truly live. Now I see it as possibly the most important thing that I have done with my life, for without it, nothing else would have been possible. The truth is that once you free yourself from addiction, a much more enjoyable and productive life than you could have imagined awaits. Here's to wishing you great success and happiness.

9 781687 564245